MW01130168

THE TANTRUM MONSTER

by Michael Gordon

THIS BOOK BELOGNS TO

....

....

"I don't want this," said Davy as he sat down to eat.

"I'm in the mood to eat something nice and sweet."

"Sweet things are for monsters who eat dinner," Mama said.

"That's not fair," said Davy, "I want ice-cream instead."

Once he'd finished dinner and ice cream, Davy went off to play.

Then Mama called him for bedtime at the end of the day.

"I'm not tired," said Davy, "I don't want to go to bed.

I'd like to stay out in the yard and play instead."

"Monsters who don't sleep get grumpy," Mama said.

"No, it's you who makes me grumpy. I'm all hot and red.

Can my friend come in too?" Davy said showing Mama a mouse.

Mama gasped, "No, Davy, you can't bring that into the house."

A grumpy Davy cleaned his teeth and got ready for bed.

Mama came in to give him cuddles while his story was read.

"I'm not sleepy, Mama, I want to get up and play."

Mama said, "Nighttime is for sleeping. You can play during the day."

Davy thought, "Why do grown-
ups always think they know best

about what you should eat
and when you should rest?

I've had enough of these
rules. They are not for me.

I'm running away. I'll do
what I want and be free."

Davy filled one bag with toys then started fillting another.

As he did so, he thought about Joey, his funny big brother.

He'd miss all the fun they have together whenever they play.

He won't be able to do that again when he runs away.

Toys packed, Davy went in search of his favorite ball in the yard.

He thought about playing ball with Dad. Leaving Dad would be hard.

Dad was so much fun. He always made Davy laugh.

They always had the very best water fights when Davy took his bath.

As Davy searched through his books looking for his favorite one,

He remembered Mama's silly voices. She made stories such fun.

He'd miss cuddles at night and story time before bed.

From now on, he'd have to read his own bedtime stories instead.

Davy would need some food to survive and lots of snacks to eat.

He remembered Mama's apple pie. She made it so nice and sweet.

He'd miss eating dinner with his family and Mama's stories at night.

Davy was angry before, but he felt calm now. Maybe leaving wasn't right.

"Although my parents' rules sometimes make me feel mad,

I know the people who love me most are Joey and my mom and dad.

I love them all," Davy thought. "We have so much fun together."

So Davy unpacked his bags because he could never leave them forever.

About author

Michael Gordon is the talented author of several highly rated children's books including the popular Sleep Tight, Little Monster, and the Animal Bedtime.

He collaborates with the renowned Kids Book Book that creates picture books for all of ages to enjoy. Michael's goal is to create books that are engaging, funny, and inspirational for children of all ages and their parents.

Contact

For all other questions about books or author, please e-mail michaelgordonclub@gmail.com.

Award-winning books

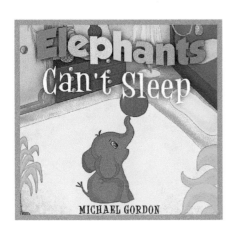

Elephants Can not Sleep

The

Little Elephant likes to break the rules. He never cleans his room. He never listens to mama's bedtime stories and goes to bed really late. But what if he tried to follow the routine so that the bedtime would become an amazing experience?

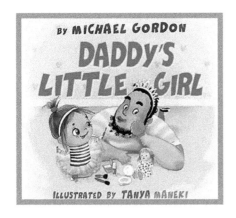

Little Girl's Daddy

the Who Needs a super hero the when you have your dad? Written in beautiful rhyme this is an excellent story that honors all fathers in the world.

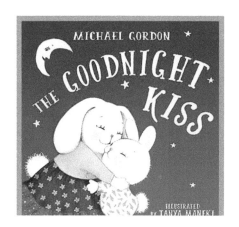

The Goodnight Kiss

Welcome to a cozy, sweet little bunny family. Mom is putting her little son Ben to bed, but she's not quite successful. Little boy still wants to play games and stay up late. Ben also likes to keep his mommy in his room at bedtime. Mrs. Bunny tries milk, warm blankets, books , and finally a kiss ... what will work?

My Big Brother

The

Each of our lives will always be a special part of the other. There's Nothing Quite Like A Sibling Bond Written in beautiful rhyme this is an excellent story that values patience, acceptance and bond between a brother and his sister.

CPSIA information can be obtained
at www.ICGtesting.com
Printed in the USA
BVHW021046290621
610723BV00009B/1986